CW00556206

An Open Mouth

poems by

W. Yusef Doucet

ATOPON BOOKS

Atopon Books
907 15th Street
Santa Monica, California 90403
United States

Copyright © 2024 by W. Yusef Doucet
All Rights Reserved.

Publisher's Cataloging-in-Publication data

Names: Doucet, W. Yusef, author.
Title: An open mouth : poems / W. Yusef Doucet.
Description: Santa Monica, CA: Atopon Books, 2024.
Identifiers: LCCN: 2023948744 | ISBN: 979-8-9866907-0-4 (paperback) |
979-8-9866907-6-6 (hardcover)
Subjects: LCSH American poetry--21st century. | American poetry--African
American authors. | BISAC / POETRY / General | POETRY / American /
African American & Black
Classification: LCC PS3604 .O63 O74 2024 | DDC 811.6--dc23

"Diaspora (para Itana)" previously published in *Root Work Journal: Convening in
the Ark*. Vol. 1 Issue 1 August 2020.

"The Aiyana Jones Villanelle" previously posted at Blackfood.org and www.
freeignace.blog. 2010

Cover Art: "Jihad" by DJ Watson

Cover Design: Otim

Printed in the United States of America.

Order of Appearance

One:
Without Sleep

Two:
Irresponsible Comments

Three:
The Personal, The Public

One:

Without Sleep

insomnia #1

No one should have been there
At that hour of morning
At La Cienega and Rodeo.
So when the plastic bag
Of cheese popcorn squealed
For attention: "look, look,
Look at him and look at her,"
The celebrity magazine
The snickers bar and the popcorn
Could not mask our real purpose:
Two raspberry wine coolers
That matched your dress
And our intentions.

So when the Ethiopian woman
Behind the counter asked me please
To repeat my request
Louder than a whisper,
Ten ears strained to hear me
Ask again for the condoms.

Still, I'm glad we left the party
Before we arrived at the party.
It is so much better to be awake
All night not alone

insomnia #2

I can fall asleep when I want to fall asleep.
then two a.m. arrives close mouthed.

rubber no longer hums down the street.
the rising whistle and falling murmur

of car engines dopplering by become
the lone whale song of busses on the hour.

they rarely stop to release their blow hole
doors open for late night riders,

dark men wearing bomber jackets
who return from secured buildings,

women reading Spanish language magazines
going to work to clean homes and children,

have to be there by five a.m.
across town. They must wake up at two.

I see them.
There should be a witness.

I can fall asleep when I want to fall asleep.
I just never want to fall asleep.

insomnia #3

The Late Show,
before talking heads
invaded night,
and stars troop
from cover to couch
mongering product,
the show that followed
Carson's trail
before stupid pets
or stupid human tricks,
when the late show
was the late, late show

The Late Show
old movies:
walking space plants
that invade earth and blind
the world but for
a brave girl
and a sailor,
or Anthony Quinn
chasing John Barrymore, Jr.
and Maureen O'Hara to Dariabar
across a gray sea shining
from the tiny box.

Sometimes a warm glow
sometimes a cold glow.

That Late Show
ignited fires.

Desire

at the party
he watches her
black curls fall
over her shoulder
when she laughs
and throws her head
back in the garden
patio under the string
of lights and through
the open kitchen door.
he sits in the living room
an endless fifty feet away
his tongue turned to stone.
he turns away when she turns
smiling delighted because
she is at a party and popular
and he knows no one really,
embarrassed to have his eyes
caught devouring her
without knowledge
or permission.

Soldier's Return

the young man in desert fatigues
quietly accepts thanks from
the mouths of grateful citizens
arrayed in defensive positions
against exploding spit
and phantom missiles from
reporters missing in action.

the young man in desert fatigues
quietly walks through the airport.
he looks at no one applauding him
in spurts of ovation, clean hands
clapping, that bear none of the red
terror he rubs off in his dreams
of heat and smoke and limbs burning

small arms like big arms
quivering in the street
at midday prayer.
These trophies few citizens
imagine in their grateful
awe and chest-warming pride.

the young man in desert fatigues
quietly embraces his comrades
waiting at the gate in desert fatigues
less tired now to be in the company
of others like him who know
despite the devotions of true believers
what the monument will not say
has to be said:
somebody killed those babies.

insomnia #4

the L.A. air at three a.m.
bites light bites

nibbles

like a favorite lover's
cold nose, teeth, and tongue

Hop scotching your torso,
half under loose sheets

playful but sharp enough
to make you shiver and

pull the robe tighter
around you

or the lover closer

Mr. Mann

Mr. Mann never once punched a man
nor wrapped angry hands around a woman's
throat to stop her screams or punish her.

Mr. Mann never shot a young groom
the night before his wedding.

Mr. Mann never raided a construction site
nor the factory where his shirts are sewn
by thousands of sinewy fingers
flying and bleeding in the stifling close air.

Mr. Mann never flew a sortie after midnight
over Baghdad, nor ordered a drone blind
across a border to dismember secret people
and people in the way of remote control fire.

Mr. Mann never dropped shield-less, cross-less
patients alone and lost on the skid row streets.

Mr. Mann does not even approve of so much grief
and shakes his head vigorously about the sad state
of crowded schools, and gangs sieging dusty neighborhoods.

What can Mr. Mann do but go to work,
take care of his own, pay his taxes and vote?
Mr. Mann always votes.

With so many problems what can one man do?
What can any of us do that we already don't?

Green Leaf

. . .Breathe in

nights in the open yard
beneath the bloom-and-fruit-
year-round orange trees,

days in the soft shade they
offer from the sun's glare
and the blare on the boulevard,

mornings in the quiet cool
bedroom, we stop to breathe
the sweet fire and smoke

and feel our heads stretch
the air and laughter settle
light at home in the gut.

Breathe out. . .

insomnia #5

eleven o'clock news readers banter
until roll credits speed and the lamps dim
in the rooms through the house, quiet and sleep
begin to blanket the walls that an hour
before bounced with life-in-action.

then my eyes brighten up, my eyebrows raise
my scalp tingles to know that silent hours
settle into a ball for the night's rest
and my second day begins before this
day ends. it is precious to me.

I am spending heartbeats to keep it mine
my time, my muted streets, my room
where I sit and listen to the noiseless
breathing from the other bedrooms
those I love who know nothing of the costs.

Clearing the Air

after rain in the Basin
they see a postcard view,
the citizens in the hills:

Spanish tile roofs stacked side
by side in rows and more trees
than common flatland views,

frozen mountains north and east
the city in daylight shines white
amidst the tableau

more beauty than collected
beneath freeway underpasses
and in the boxes

side by side to south and east
ordinarily masked
by air thicker than water

that now, after showers,
draws back its veil to offer
its favors to favored

vistas unfamiliar
with the stains left behind
on the flatland avenues

or the stench when their shit
rolls downhill in the runoff
from overstuffed toilets.

insomnia #6

even though my body aches,

stones tumble down the muscle
on either side of my spine
and settle like jagged boulders
in the small of my back,

my legs strain to keep me
on my feet crumbling beneath
the weight of the hours,

my wrists burn where the pulse
beats a fevered rhythm into my hands
until they throb and shake,

my whole body trembles
until I go ahead
and lie down in the dark

still awake
while my mind races
and I watch the horses run.

I Know How You Mean to Love Me

come to my room in dark light
and undress me with your smile.

your skin still smells of mango.
my nose breathes your scent deeply

along the line of your neck.
I feel lips leave light kisses

across my chest and stomach
a feathered torture, breathless

my body the flesh fevered
holds you close in my arms like
a falling man clings to air,

we two fighting to be one body.

insomnia #7

the nights you sleep at home
and not in this bed, where

your scent and random strands
of your hair, your impression

in the mattress and the sheet
pulled slightly to your side

offer none of the comfort
nor the warmth that your body

offers, languid, asleep early
and lean into me from beneath

the covers and in the middle
of the bed, those nights you sleep

at home, I have no reason to go to bed.
I'll sleep eventually.

The Mortician's Missive

Dear Mr. President:
Although the surge
in business has stacked
the bottom line,
the business never
suffers as there is always
a supply of product,
this unpleasantness
being nature's way and all.
Honestly, we don't easily
grow accustomed to so many
parents burying their children.
We prefer our clients youngish,
easing their farewells to the old.
But the old burying the young?
Well, sir, it's a bit unseemly,
don't you think, just not the way
of things. So, profit margins
and all aside, we'd just as well
do without the surge.
Thank you, no.

insomnia #8

there is a warmth in moments
when the dark and silent late
hours turn their faces
to the dark, silent early hours

and monks rise from cots
for morning prayers and work
for their hands in dough or earth
lest they be idle.

hedonists fold into beds
for sleep finally, or trysts,
their desperate limbs tangled,
lest they be idle too.

Pookie Got Feelin's Too

jus' cuz I got popped ridin' dirty
don' mean I couldn't care for my boo.

my baby ain't have to grow up wonderin'
where his daddy is. Shit, I worked,

and I didn' bang, not like no real gangstas.
juvenile paper suppose to be closed anyway.

What I make at two jobs movin' boxes
don' buy milk and medicine

and my girl doin' her thang at the beauty parlor,
so when baby boy cryin'

a man got to do something. I ain't turnin'
my girl out on the track.

So I try to move a little plant
in the 'hood, some little "feel good"

for the people. now you talkin' 'bout me
like I'm a dog don't know what it means

to live without a daddy cuz he was popped
on stupid shit too. you act like my heart

don' splinter when I think that my boy
will have to lie when at school he get asked

what his daddy do. and his mama, my boo,
what she gon' have to do?

the words taste bitter in my mouth
to tell her not to wait for me.

Yeah, I was ridin' a little dirty.
But who makin' the real money

From seed to baggy, leaf to powder
And bodies for beds to boot?

WWFS

"probably something anti-semitic"
a gray haired maybe jewish woman
says like she knows him. I don't
see the voice answer the question
posed on my tee shirt:
What Would Farrakhan Say?
I find it a strange thing to hear
doing groceries and look up
I see her and smile before I realize
she's answering my tee shirt's question
she smiles back, surprised, her sword
drops, mine never drawn, I thought.
There is a valley between us.
we could talk about art
and the designer's ironic smile.
she wiggles in the smiling silence
and asks me if I think so:
"don't you think so?"

no, I don't think so, "probably not"
I say and push my cart away.
still smiling.

insomnia #9

awake some spring nights
at four, the street barely breathes,
the air, electric.

It's in How You Define the Problem

the neighborhood council
puts it to a vote:

shall we or shall we not
require parking permits?

with what other sandbag
can we dam the flow

of people sleeping in
their cars on our blocks

when they threaten to flood
our tree-lined fortress?

Conditions for Negotiation

when throats open to sing songs new
of human rights and the human spirit,

when the champions of conscience
laud lost heroes holed in dark places,

detained for actions deemed harmful
to nation, state and people,

when voices west of east and north of poor
cry outrage at power's contempt

for the democratic right to vote in free
and fair elections for our betters,

perhaps they will remember that
their high ideals have not kept

the prison yards nor pockets empty.
perhaps they will remember that

panthers carry consciences too.
perhaps they will remember me.

insomnia #10

I watch the water
spot slip across the
bedroom ceiling in
concentric brown rings.

if it were a tree
still, it would be three
years old, the number
of years in night times

I have watched a planet form.

A Bullet in Three Haikus

bullet in barrel,
does he think about paying
the cost of living?

bullet burns the air;
did he understand in time
the price for fighting?

bullet through his head,
had he considered before
a higher price paid?

RSVP

the invitation to dinner
long arriving in the mail

when all you had to do was stick
your head into the kitchen
or the custodians' closet
or the maids' quarters,
or the detention rooms,

the invitation is appreciated,
but I would just as well eat
in the kitchen with the rest
of the help, even despite
the seat at the table's head.

I can see how important to you
sharing the table is now.
still, some of us don't dream
of dinner in the suburbs.
the simple company of comrades
and a dinner of beans and rice,
these will suffice.

revolting

pictures of marchers flicker in live color,
but mostly white, on the television.
american flags don't-tread-on-me wave
in gloved and mittened hands
these patriots dumping teabags
into the dry harbors of suburban streets
sprawled across the country
dutiful soldiers so loudly declare
they will it take back.

from whom? who took it from them? when?

meanwhile, gun sales continue to rise.

insomnia #11

four o'clock again.
a possum crosses the yard
north tree to south tree.

Overheard a Poem

in a cold, hungry
weakened world

the corpses lie
piled beneath

glimmering words
embossed in gold

thread sewn in satin
pillows, and

gold leaf beaten fine
in marble.

insomnia #12

criminals in suits
conspire to deprive me
of dreams with flat shadows.

For the Linger

when you wrap
your legs

around my waist,
I pull

you to my chest
the chest

you kissed with
your tongue

I pull you close
to breathe

your scent deep
and try

to move through you
to smell

your skin and taste
you on

my lips through
the day.

insomnia #13

the nights I get home late
the dark shines like the day
if there is to be for me
any hours I claim my own.

my face to a screen
the television lies.
it is during the night
that I lay my mind to rest.

insomnia #14

Do you hear me call your name
at night in bed with emptiness?
Does a night breeze catch the words
and carry them to the street,
and they turn into lizards?
Does a night bird spy them running
fast across the pavement,
searching for a path to your ears
to drop precious whispers in them?
an owl that swoops them up and flies to your home
where the words struggle and are dropped
at your window, tapping?

And you in repose.

Do you hear me repeat your name,
hear me hug blanket, embrace longing
spend the night imagining the dark imprints
we leave in the sand wet after tides and crowds
of children and their haggard mamas and papas?
I rub my hands over my face, washing it
with imaginary sea water; I inhale my fingers
where they should smell of you,
kiss my fingers, wish they tasted of you.

And you in smiling sleep.

After Thoughts

a story in the corner
of the near back pages
of the newspaper reports
five soldiers dead

another war abroad
another roadside bomb
another drone attack
it sounds almost exotic,

muted on the news channels
for weeks and months
as war becomes mundane
mundane enough to be a story

in the bottom corner
of the near back pages
periodic human tragedies
and perhaps select coverage

of a president saluting
flag wrapped caskets
on the tarmac for a people
grown used to silence.

Two:

Irresponsible Comments

Water

Now we use pliers to turn on the shower.
And the water flows in warm sheets
Light tropical rains at the command
Of hands nimble enough to grip the handles
And turn and believe that water should flow.

We don't drink the water we use to wash
Our bodies and dishes and delicate fabrics.
We don't walk five miles to the river or wadi
Then five miles back head bearing gallons
To a place without pipes and spigots

The water we drink costs twenty cents
Per gallon at the supermarket water machine—
Much less in the sweat exchange—
The city treats the water from the pipes
And we treat it again asking, "Is it clean?

What have They put in it? Is this Flint?
Is this a Third World Country?" No,
It's a Third World neighborhood
In a north world country, so even if crumbling,
The plumbing mostly works.

Solitary

Neither the knots in the mattress
Nor the springs searching the narrow
Between my back and the metal cot
Nor the dark that lives in this hole
Longer than any man shelved here
Unless he should spread contagion
To the minds of poor men jailed.

What makes the dark and stink two things
Unbearable, a great club to break
My back and a hook to tear the sinews
From my bones soaking the cold cement
Into their resolve, their old iron bent
By dim forgetfulness made habit:
My people have no memory of me,

Nor the hundreds like me imprisoned
Because we dare love Black people
More than a stock portfolio,
An office off Harvard Square,
A chance to be sheriff or mayor
Of some southern town or northern city,
Or a star shining in the west of hell.

Insatiable

He sits in the chair and watches
The Vietnamese woman work his nails
With a silversmith's skills and wonders
At what cost he could mine her ore
With a blunter tool unused to detail
Work or the precise traffic of fingers
Over expensive palms.
Through hair, skin and sweat beaded
And glistening at her temples
He wants to taste her temple

Remove a lock of hair from her ear
And whisper burning words
That will make her tan cheeks flush
And smile at him with promise.
Her hands soothe his hands
And brush away the flakes of bone and flesh
Left behind from his work on the stock market.
He eyes her forearms twitch
His mouth moistens

She works, dreaming of him drowning
In a bitter pool of his own spit.

Zombie #1

When did he steal your soul, zombie?
What wicked sorcerer drained you?
Poured your soul out, a libation
And offering, slow, sweet and black
For the dead who eat the dead and
Never grow full, some dark rum for
The bloodless devils that live in
The emptiness left within you?

Zombie, look at you. Can you see
Your reflection in a pool of rain
Water or a mirror when your
Stolen soul is not your own soul?
Does a dead man watch from the glass?
Can he see you fade into ash?
What rider drives your head, zombie
And makes you think you alone drive?

In the Dark

I must face it
The galling truth
Of my own self
That in the dark
Under cover
Of a blanket
Of velvet black
Too dark to see
My outstretched hand,
And even in
The company
Of dear strangers,
My thoughts sometimes
Turn quite bloody:

The man living
In the pictures
Inside my head
Bites his lip and
Wraps his fingers
Iron gripped tight
Around the throat
Of an ashen
Faced man in blue
Collars and bars
Sewn on the sleeves
Before its mouth
Can open and
Swallow him whole.

The News from L.A., U.S.A.

In L.A.
this is what it means to die:
one man and one needle
one bag of heroin and the life that pinches too sharply.

Two men and the same needle
another bag of skag.
A man, a woman, his wife.
No needle, no dope, a secret
and no condom.

This is what it means:
a young man with a gun,
his swagger and armor
against his shaking inside.

Two young men and more guns
ride in search of hurt.

Another young man, he stands
in his yard. He never saw
the fire fly through him.

In his house, his sister bleeds
where the bullet tears her skin,
and frightened boys retreat
to a life squeezed between despair and rage.

Malt liquor and weed can't
quiet the screens.

The young man, his girlfriend,
not enough dope in the world,
 and no condom.

This is what it means:
a black and white, a flashing light,
a teenager at the wheel moves too slow
or too abrupt.

Two drawn guns standard issue,
he never sees the holding cell.

A man reads about it in his daily paper.
Such a shame, he says,
a horrible waste of life, he says,

black boy's life ain't worth a damn, he says.
He folds the paper and shakes his head.
 His wife feeds him
fried pork chops and gravy

because she loves him,
and he loves smothered pork chops.

He eats alone. She sits alone
with a cigarette and the secret
in the kitchen. And no condom.

One heart, one soul alone,
one kitchen, one house,
one neighborhood at a time,
this is what it means
to die in LA.

Lunch in the Quarter

It was funny how we both felt.
The mopped vomit and tequila still
Swung on the air down Bourbon Street
Like a lingering ill breath.
We had to get off Bourbon,
Walk back to Chartres and away
From short-panted revelers draped over
The wrought iron metal work
Of African hands intimate with Ogun,
Short pants hanging from the doors
Of colonial buildings built
By branded men and women.
We were invisible to them.

We wanted them gone.
You called them invaders, and we
Visitors in the home of our fathers
Felt ourselves drowning among them.
We were invisible to them:
Une métisse tragique
And a runaway slave
Loose in the quarter and together
Planning rebellion over beans and rice, listening for the Congo
drums.
We have always been invisible to them.
That's our power

Geometry

The hour arrives softly at my shoulder.
Just to my left and in the corner of my eye.
I see the hour's hand reach to tap me
Tap me twice, a reminder to breathe,
To inhale the night, and bless the quiet

Then I stretch my hand just to my left
Where my pipe sits, blown blue glass
With a star on the end, or a flower
It depends how you see it, at what angle
The herb has described you

Around a point in space.

Diaspora (*para Itana*)

Thousands more miles separated a little black girl
At play with red chickens in her grandma's yard
In Salvador, Bahia, and the black boy throwing a baseball
Against the red brick wall in his Los Angeles backyard.

Why should distance matter?
Why should language matter?
"When you speak, I know you in my spirit,
In my spirit right here."

She speaks with her hand over her heart.
Why should distance matter?
Why should language matter?
"I'm so glad," he says. "I've known you

My whole life, in my heart right here.
I could hear you giggle when the baseball
Bounced back and your delight
Would scatter the chickens."

The Right to Fail

We sleep on pavement,
Sun and wind burned faces.
We collect half-eaten
Sandwiches from garbage cans.

We wait in emergency rooms
For flu shots and gun shots.
A night in county lock-up
Is a favor sometimes.

The man on the news we watch
On the motel wall reminds us
We are civilized and lucky to live
In a great nation, a generous country

When private security moves us along
Before the patrons can see us
Or smell the reek of freedom
Four weeks under sun and stars
Since our last county shower

Zombie #2

New boots cross the waxed floor.
He looks down and sees his face
Clean shaven, brown and bending
Beneath the rubber soles.

He pushes the corners of his lips
Down to hide the joy that pricks
His skin. Delighted to be under
The eyes of grateful civilians,

He can feel his pants fabric stiffen
At the thought of rapid discharges
And the recruiter's promise of
All the foreign pussy he can fuck.

New Orleans East

I asked my cousin if their house flooded.
"Oh yeah," she said. "The water
Came up to here." Her hand level
With the black marble countertop
In the kitchen. We ate red beans
And rice and baked chicken
And some sweet, sweet ice-tea
Before bed. In the morning
I looked out the bedroom window
And saw the canal running behind
The house. Ducks and a heron
Stalked the stretch passing the yard
Fishing in a shallow current.
I could see the bottom. I could see
The water rise and flood the house
As high as the black marble counters.
We could see the lake off the freeway.

"You all see the hospital still closed.
That was the only hospital around here
Without having to get on the freeway.
They gonna keep it closed. And it's
Good luck, y'all."

Zombie #3

They build castles on bone pits
Spread great green parks over graves
Power cities in deserts
Fueled by dams and rivers
Where bodies float in toxic streams,
They paint their skins in gold dust
Still the hunger never slakes
And then they suffocate.

Emblems

You wear me on your wrist
A lucky charm against the dark
To keep the ganging shades across town
Lodged between alleys and grated windows

You keep me your secret wish to embrace a phantom
And love the caresses of dark men and women,
The dark one who whispers in your ear
A dark body to bear your shame and lashes

You paint my profile on old family crests,
A token of wealth for the moneyed democracies,
A court pet, exotic and Moorish,
Erudite, sophisticated, comforting and gelded

You believe me the boogey man beneath your bed
The monster on the corner, crazed dictator, unfit parent,
Disease carrier, what's-wrong-with-the-country,
You poster walls and screens with my face:

Most wanted and most starving
You wear me like the bangles you swing from your limbs
And hang me from the neck, a black body crucified
On the milky breast of an American matron

Hugging the Coast

Here I stand
This west coast beach
Edge of a continent
Lip of an empire
I look west to see east
And wonder:

How many other black men
And otherwise black men of a middle age
Walk a beach and think
The things I am thinking

About beaches
And men with guns
And how long one might expect to live
To survive crossfire, police, D.A.s, unemployment,
Bad health, worse habits, traffic, sex, each other;

I want to reach across the Pacific
And take some brother's hand
I want to share his load
Work alongside him
In the field, on the mountain
In the burning streets

I'll be a man who can breathe
Underwater like a fish-man
I'll walk under the waves
Fight the current pushing me back
Slice deeper into the water, into the dark

But the pressure becomes too much
My chest flattens
I can't be a man who breathes
Underwater

So I'll be a man who can walk on water
I'll stride the cold Pacific waves
Past the oil tankers, past the trawlers
Past the aircraft carriers
Invisible to their radar
A strange porpoise

And when I see land
See men and women on the shore
Waving their arms and shouting
But it's not joy, it's not welcome
Instead they grab me call me heretic
And tear me to pieces in a religious ecstasy.

No, I can't be a man who walks on water
So I turn around and look east
To see midwest
Where people love a Jesus I don't know,
One who does not dance at weddings
Nor dine with publicans and prostitutes
And overturn moneychangers' tables.

So I will stand here
I will sit here
I will lie here in the sand
On the lip of an empire
I will stretch out my arms and hug the beach.
I will wait for my brother's hand

And for my sister's hand too
From across the ocean and the continent's spine

And still maybe have a chance to hold a woman
And love her enough to live
And to live better.

Still Life

In a bare room
A black bowl sits
Full with space and
A hairline crack.

Aiyana Jones Villanelle (For Aiyana Stanley-Jones)

A gun metal May night she lies safe asleep in her bed
While down the street a war descends on the room
Detroit police with the missile that flies at her head.

A little girl seven years old dreams of the book she read,
Did she hear glass shatter, the boots kick doors, or the boom
And flash of the grenade as she lay safe asleep in her bed?

The coroner said the bullet blasted her head
And the bullet cut her neck before she knew her doom,
When they fired the bullet through the air at her head.

It was the wrong apartment, but one must not be misled.
The S.W.A.T. team knew they might have the wrong room
A gun metal May night she lay safe asleep in her bed.

But was it their fault the living room couch was her bed?
In a rich country like theirs, how were they to assume
A Detroit police bullet would blast her young head?

So outraged again we place candles at the door where she bled,
Where grandmothers and granddaughters sleep and live in one room
Where they thought she lay that May night safe asleep in her bed
And the Detroit police opened her seven-year-old head.

They Look Like Us

Their eyes are brown and round
or shaped like almonds.
They look through paneless windows
at the stones that are not loaves.
They cannot eat them,
 so they throw them at tanks
and swallow fire.
They look like us.

Their eyes are large and wet
and streak their brown cheeks.
salty and red streams run
to the corners of their mouths,
bitter water they cannot swallow,
so they spit sorrow with teeth and nails to the floor.
They look like us.

Their mouths are brown and pink
and full of a clamoring hush.
It screams in their throats,
chokes their words back.
So they smash their fists
against cement walls, chip stone, smash bone
to feel.

Like us,
their stomachs are loud and swollen,
and their hunger drags their legs.
When daddies come home from day labor
and mommies come home from sweat labor,
some cannot hold them and feed them,
so some feed them, and the babies feel full but unwanted.

Some cannot feed them and hold them,
so some hold them, and the babies feel wanted but hungry.

Like us, they rage.
Like us, they bleed.
Their hearts crack like cold stones,
imperfect diamonds refracting light
drained of color and fire.
A shadow crawls on the hardening veins.
Like us, their hearts break open.
And the fruit rots
to the core
the core turns to stones,
stones to throw at tanks.

La chanson pour les genocidaires

Millions dead beneath the seas
Millions more bear disease
Swollen bellies, pocked scarred faces
Unnatural bleeding from private places

A million cops patrol the streets
A million perps beneath the sheets
One million five in prison beds,
Concrete pillows for a million heads.

A million babies for the Spanish hounds
A million families in the shanty towns
A million children see only strife
A million throats feel the blade of the knife.
Millions of folks don't know why.
Who told the lie?
Why did they die?

A million more cases of AIDS
A million grandmothers pull down their shades
A million babies that won't be born
A million condoms that should've been worn

A million men hanging from ropes
A million addicts using to cope
A million women kicked in the gut,
Punched in the mouth, called a whore slut.
A million civilian lives to be saved
A million civilians bombed to their graves
A million gallons of toxic waste poured
A million pirates shot off their shore

Millions of people want to know why
Who told the lie?
Why do we die?

A million shadows burned in the wall
Depleted uranium fired and falls
A million grains of toxic sand
A million years of poisoned land
Millions of people want to know why
Who told the lie?
Why do we die?

Whose hands
Commit the crime?
Whose juries
Steal the time?
Whose soldiers
Run and hide?
When do we call it
Genocide?

Stigmata

"...no gentleness can efface the marks of violence.
Only violence can itself destroy them."

  - Frantz Fanon

Most settlers have never seen their fathers' violence
waste human beings, nor the regular police
terror in the native quarters of the city.
What desperate acts collide with celluloid fantasy
Aryan polemics in the rush to expose a fascist ecstasy...
blinded aggression binds together psyches under siege.
The marks of violence fill the gray-spaced
inner city uncertainties with certain anxieties.
Native youth live conflict. Fury spins
their Gats on their Glocks, makes the native quarters
a dangerous place, makes the quarters
Manichean constructs by supremacists:
a postcard from a Soweto schoolyard,
the moral prerequisite that evil be
stamped out in all its objective forms,
the black battalions most efficient in the march
to free civilization of them native citizen selves,
washed white in the ritual blood letting
 of familiar combat.

Poteau-mitan

like they are the centers of the known world:
the unknown of oceans and caves,
the aromas of soils, softly along her bends and richly,
it is warm and deep, drips moisture for the living,
it is furnace, and mystery forest,
the fear that compels the frightened to stare.

like they are the centers of the known world:
feeling the furry maw swallow the little sun
arouses the flow rushing through his members
straining the walls, terrified by the rapture
of imminent death... is that the sun
bursting in her veins and her belly radiating?

like they are the centers of the known world:
terror, terror, the sun is plundered!

Three:
The Personal, The Public

resisting forgetfulness

Jackboot futures up on the market,
The trade in riot gear is brisk.
Global market forces assault
The villages of our hearts our
memory of local life

Zapatistas dancing on the lip of a volcano
point the way to freedom

Who could prophesy
A Republic so far flung,
Expert imperium, exquisite discipline,
Cruel elegance;
What silent Sybil could foresee
 A Pox Americana,

or Zapatistas dancing in the mouth of a volcano?

Across the narrow waist of turtle island.
What secreted maneuvers
Follow Conquistador footprints?
When the American legions hump through Andean sky
Reconnoiter Amazon headwaters,
Secure the Cordillera

Do they consider the soul of Machu Picchu,
Or the science of Copan?

Do they consider in the north
Zapatistas dancing down the sides of the volcano
Zapatistas dancing in the burning blood of earth
rolling down the mountain
rolling through the valley
rolling through our spirits
from the mouth of the volcano?

The Fall

I sat radiant in a star
bronzed in its gut
when the singularity of opal black
eyes pulled me to their event horizon.
I flung myself
into cold space hurtled
heated the empty between
slapped by comets' tails.

Now my trajectory draws me to the blue
planet on the nail of a spiral galaxy's finger
I enter the atmosphere
and the atmosphere does not burn me
a burning star man aimed
for the irresistible urge of earth
leaping to embrace my dive

an earth of black-eyed angels
stokes the blaze of possibilities
to catch me in my leap
of head and heart and arms and legs
spread and reaching
looking for a falling star man

for those sable eyes
I abandoned my star
I leapt to be caught
in her arms to
land my lips on her lips
disintegrate in the embrace
of her singularity.

or crash.

Blue

she wore blue jeans and a blue embroidered
cotton blouse, its fluted sleeves flowing down
her slender wrists and hands like blue streams
flowing over smooth, brown, narrow stones.
the blouse rippled like the surface of a
freshwater pond, her face a mystery
framed by a waterfall of black curls,
a mystery I wanted to enter.
she wore blue like Yemaya's devotees
blue my favorite color, I would tell her
that we both noticed, Yemaya and I.
I would kiss her for it if I could,
I would kiss her for the thought.

Offering

Your eyes, obsidian daggers, cut
out my heart an offering of sinew and heat
for the vines and flowers of your hair,

your hands and feet are hummingbirds,
your arms and legs are gazelles,
your breasts are leaping fawns

a singing stream your voice
Your lips, the shrine where
I would place a burning tongue

a flame at play with a flame
Your lap the altar, there I place a ruby
warm and beating, where I would place pearls,

Your left hand resting on them
Your right hand raised to heaven
The *Xochitl*, opening.

Industry

he tears through the forest
rips the growth from its roots,
furiously turns the soils
strips and strips the layers away
leaves streaks of her blood smeared mercilessly
over her bruised and abraded thighs
he, fascinated with his power to hurt
what he fears, uses it to steal the earth
and fears it still.

Grandmother's Kitchen

Always…
a pot of rice on the stove
the scent of okra cooking,
chopped onion, celery, and bell pepper,
yesterday today tomorrow,
everyday so when someone anyone
everyone brings a body by
to see "how ya mama 'n 'em doing"
she could feed a body food
while she feeds a soul comfort
And maybe have Poppa
send Unc' to the corner store
so folks can have taste…always

The Best People

So often the best
people are the worst people
in the whole wide world.

Visitation

A spider lives between spaces
between the sections of my desk.
A hawk perched on the balcony
outside my window.

Anansi in the house
Heru outside
I cannot say what message they bring
but take the signs to heart as blessing.

The One so small
Acquainted with secret spaces
The One so big
Master of the wide sky

Creator
Sustainer
Spinning webs of my life
Lifting my spirit

So I guess
the message
is connect
and fly.

With You (for Tasha)

The plainest words
ordinary like air
warmed in the sun
wrapped around
our everyday
solar blood breathed
through the skin the fuel
to keep us going
like the words
that keep me going:

"I'm on your side,
Black man."

Time and Distance

I miss you,
the satin pleasures
of your skin
feather fine hairs
electric under my touch
fingers that run the length
and curves of your legs…

Voluptuous
my earth goddess
full fertile brain
wide and deep
as the ocean of space
cradle of stars
radiant against the full
emptiness of your absence…

I
 miss
      you…

Crows Among the Jacaranda

The spring midday sky disappears
above a bright lavender canopy.
a sea road of purple petals unfolds
beneath that amethyst sky
where winged shadows dart
through the pink clouds
and hop among the branches
of the tall jacaranda trees.

Climate

It is a matter of degrees
On a planet ideally situated
You waited
between sun fire
And space ice

To fling life on top of life
at the rate a mountain rises
Fragile fortunate balance.

I will be warm tonight.
The man sleeping on
the sidewalk will shiver.

An indelicate imbalance
An industrial strength greed
heating and freezing
The life out of Life.

Sacred Hearts

Seven fall eggplants grew from
Six plants in the summer garden,
most after brown had crept up
the green stalks of the tomato
and squash plants.
Chapped hands pick the tear drop
Gourds wondering whether weeding
would win us more purple fruit
the shape of human hearts
and able to fit in the hand
fingers wrapped around to feel
the eggplant cool and smooth
and crowned with green spikes
that stab a heart crowned in thorns
taking a sharp price in blood
to put food on the table.

Mad Ravings of the Black Petty Bourgeoisie

"What have we to fear
from the gentry's return,
we professional owners?
The flatlands? Rising rents?

Great prospects for increase…
How they gonna gentrify
what's already gentrified?"
But they did it

for a mess of pottage.
He asked the room
for a definition.
the man said Black removal.

Random Thoughts Haiku

We all disappear
in the cold absence of light,
and in its hot flood.

A Poem about Love

The people say
Love will find a way
And I love you but can't
Find a way into your heart
nor your room

The singer sang
Love is all you need
And you love me
But I need you to touch me
Wrap me kiss me
hungrily

The writer wrote
Love conquers all
And I love you still
Despite the shame
Of my defeat

Someone not knowing
Sally's song said
Love makes the world go around
And you love me
But won't come around
To my way of feeling

The singer sang
Love is stronger than death
And I love you
And I will still love you

When death embraces me
But is life stronger than love?

And you love me.
I lie unwrapped, alone
Loving you hard as I can
Across miles and days
Stroke the empty sheet
Where you would lie
When love makes a way.

The Romantic said
Love is never having to say "I'm sorry"
And I love you
And I am sorry that
My love would fill the sky
And that may be
Too much love
To fill you.

Rehabilitation Center Pick-up

Winter valley blossoms crown
Ventura Boulevard trees
fragrant cotton candy
blooms, playgrounds
for hummingbirds
and bees.

Cosmic Love Haiku

The sweet joy of life
A swift moment stretched to hold
A full universe.

New Skin

new scars
new burns
new micro
tears flesh
bears, new
sunspots
new bruise
new pain
bold art
cold sin
hard lost
hard won
torn skin
new again

The Quantum Entanglement of Water

Every handshake every pat on the back
every intimate embrace every ride
pressed among strangers on the bus
or the train or the nightclub floor
every air of mingled breath
all the bodies in contest

I watch the stream wash the atoms
of my DNA down the shower drain
small hairs imperceptible flecks of skin
the same water that knew me
when some other time some other where
I splashed and reveled in the simple pleasure
of a body in water.

War Is Our Way of Life

"War is our way of life, normal
More regular than the busses
Dependable as the year round
Orange blossoms exploding
In Southern California backyards
Standard like opening day flyovers
Before the first pitch or kickoff
Thrilling the crowd with acrobatic speed
Defying the logic of massive machines
The force rippling through the thousand bodies
The same jet fighters that keep towns
Employed and senators in office,
Jet fighters from military bases
That give towns markets and malls
Where the citizens can buy jungle
Camouflage bikes for the children
For the adults, haute couture
Desert camo Tees.
Another missile launch
Barely makes the news
No special announcement
During the game, not even
A chyron crawls
Across the screen bottom,
Just the latest scores and a reminder
That this update is brought to us
By the Army, we thank them
For their service:
For the gasoline priced below
The cost in ozone
For the coltan to cool
Our smart phones

For the extra weaponry
Our police departments enjoy
For the coffee we buy
At a price low enough
to keep the small farm family
Flush in tire tread sandals
Maybe even enough money to send
One child to school, maybe the oldest boy,
The one working on the American base,
Now that the factory where he swept floors
Lies in a pile of beams and rubble
After the last humanitarian mission
From a peace-loving people ever ready
To prove their love for peace
With as many bodies, ours and theirs,
 We need pile."

About the Author

Born and raised in Los Angeles, W. Yusef Doucet has been a life-long Californian. He co-founded and facilitated the Dyamsay Writers' Workshop with DJ Watson in Santa Monica, CA, the Third Root Writers' Workshop with Lisa Marie Rollins in Pomona, CA, a poetry reading series at the former Velocity Café with Edgar Montgomery in Santa Monica, CA, and produced seasonal readings and performances at the City Market of Los Angeles Gallery, all projects of the Ubwenge Artists Collective (co-founded with DJ Watson and Lisa Marie Rollins). He also co-programmed and co-hosted Liberation Cinema!, a monthly film screening at the AFIBA Center in South Los Angeles until the 2020 COVID-19 pandemic. Yusef is also currently a member of the Joko Collective, a grassroots community education project (check them out on YouTube and Instagram). He has been a faculty member of the Santa Monica College English Department since 1999.

Milton Keynes UK
Ingram Content Group UK Ltd.
UKHW010853280324
440101UK00001B/238

9 798986 690704